THIS BOOK BELONGS TO

Published by Sweet Cherry Publishing Limited
Unit 36, Vulcan House,
Vulcan Road,
Leicester, LE5 3EF
United Kingdom

Published in 2019

2 4 6 8 10 9 7 5 3 1

ISBN: 978-1-78226-617-4

Written by Gemma Barder

Printed and manufactured in Turkey
T.I O006

AN OFFICIAL GUIDE TO ...

THE NEXT STEP

CONTENTS

PAGE 7 : Welcome to The Next Step

PAGE 8 : Meet Noah

PAGE 9 : Meet Piper

PAGE 10 : Who Said That?

PAGE 11 : Plan the Next Step's Show

PAGE 12 : Noah's Dilemma, Part One

PAGE 14 : Find Your Perfect Duet Partner

PAGE 16 : All About Contemporary

PAGE 18 : Discover the World's Dance Legends

PAGE 20 : Meet Henry

PAGE 21 : Meet Richelle

PAGE 22 : Noah's Dilemma, Part Two

PAGE 24 : Step-By-Step Hair Tutorials

PAGE 26 : All About Hip-Hop

PAGE 28 : Find Your Place in the Team

PAGE 30 : Meet Ozzy

PAGE 31 : Meet Kenzie

PAGE 32 : Create Your Next Step Name

PAGE 33 : What's Your Future at The Next Step?

PAGE 34 : Make Your Own Super Smoothies

PAGE 36 : How to Dress to Impress

PAGE 38 : Meet Kingston

PAGE 39 : Meet Jacquie

PAGE 40 : Noah's Dilemma, Part Three

PAGE 42 : All About Ballet

PAGE 44 : Make Your Own Energy Bites

PAGE 46 : Discover Your Dance Destiny

PAGE 48 : Meet Finn

PAGE 49 : Meet Amy

PAGE 50 : Make-Up Masterclass

PAGE 52 : Dance Dares!

PAGE 54 : Name Your Next Step Troupe

PAGE 55 : Dancing and Me

PAGE 56 : Did You Know These Dance Facts?

PAGE 58 : Find Which Dance Style Suits You

PAGE 60 : Meet Summer

PAGE 61 : Meet Michelle and Emily

PAGE 62 : Noah's Dilemma, Part Four

PAGE 64 : All About Acrobatics

PAGE 66 : Time for a Cool Down

PAGE 68 : How Well Do You Know The Next Step?

THE NEXT STEP

IF YOU LOVE THE NEXT STEP AND WANT TO FIND OUT EVEN MORE ABOUT YOUR FAVOURITE DANCERS, YOU'VE PICKED UP THE RIGHT BOOK!

A-TROUPE

The Next Step would be nothing without its amazing troupe of dancers. The current A-Troupe are a mix of long-time members, who have worked their way up from J-Troupe, and brand new dancers brought in to shake things up.

SPACE TO DANCE

The Next Step Dance Studio is in Toronto and owned by Miss Kate. Studio A is the main rehearsal room for The Next Step dancers. If they need some time away from Studio A they can move into Studio 1, a smaller space that's perfect for planning routines in. Studio 1 can also be hired out by other dance troupes.

WHAT'S THE STORY?

It's the dream of any A-Trouper to go to Regionals, Nationals and maybe even Internationals, but it's going to take a lot of work to get there. If it's not a crazy Studio Head causing problems, it's a fight for a first-row spot or a studio love triangle. Whatever happens, life is never dull at The Next Step!

WHO'S IN CHARGE?

Emily and Michelle have had a few ups and downs on their way to becoming joint Studio Heads, but now they are perfectly placed to deal with anything that is thrown at them. With Emily's flair for business and Michelle's calm creativity, they are the heart and head of the studio.

TIME TO CHILL

When the troupe need to wind down or re-energise they head down to Shakes and Ladders – a board game-themed café.

SO PUT ON THOSE LEG WARMERS, WHIZZ UP A SMOOTHIE, AND GET STUCK IN!

IT'S NOAH!

HE'S THE HEART OF THE NEXT STEP AND HAS BEEN THROUGH IT ALL.

Noah has been at The Next Step for a long time. He started out in J-Troupe and, despite working hard and desperately trying his best, he was always seen as goofy and over-eager. Over time, he worked his way into A-Troupe, helped the studio to win Internationals and even became Dance Captain.

Perhaps because he's been through so much during his time at the studio, or perhaps because he's just such a genuinely nice guy, the rest of the troupe always go to him for advice. But being the eldest and most experienced dancer comes with its fair share of troubles, too. How long will Noah stay at The Next Step before moving on?

FRIENDS

NOAH is friends with everyone, especially **RICHELLE** and **HENRY**, and he's now found happiness with his girlfriend **JACQUIE**.

DID YOU KNOW?

Noah's grandparents are Italian.

Noah can sense things without seeing them, which made him perfect to step up and lead A-Troupe's blindfolded routine – a tricky challenge set to each team at Internationals. He's also pretty awesome at catching glasses of milk without spilling a drop!

FACT FILE

EYE COLOUR: Green

HAIR COLOUR: Light brown

MOST LIKELY TO: Do his best for the studio

LEAST LIKELY TO: Give up on anyone

FAVOURITE DANCE STYLE: Contemporary

SHE MIGHT BE SMALL, BUT SHE'S A MIGHTY DANCER!

Piper is James's little sister. She didn't audition for The Next Step until James had left the studio as she was scared of dancing in her big brother's shadow. She had nothing to worry about, though. Piper aced her audition and bagged herself a spot on A-Troupe, just like her big bro.

Although she is small, she is a skilled dancer and is determined to work hard to keep her spot in the troupe. Piper sometimes struggles with self-doubt, especially when she is under pressure at a competition, but she always tries her best. She is a loyal friend and sister and has a strong belief in what's right.

DID YOU KNOW?

Piper was one of the founding members of the Zero Percent Club, with Cassie, Sloane and Amy. The girls were really nervous on their first day in A-Troupe and vowed to each other that they would get their nervousness down to 0%!

Piper and James have two older sisters, although they have never been to the studio.

HEY, PIPER!

WHO SAID THAT?

The dancers at The Next Step have a lot to say. Can you match the quote to the dancer?

1 'I think Dance Detention is like a jail they put you in when you commit crimes against dance.' *Ozzy*

2 'I can't believe I just blew it for the team. I let Miss Angela get into my head.' *Piper*

3 'Kenzie is going to be mad at me forever, but it's not my fault!' *Jacquie*

4 'Escape room? Fun! This is exactly what the team needs.' *Amy*

5 'Usually I try to see the good in everybody, but with Lily, she always has a hidden motive.' *Kenzie*

6 'I'm not surprised that I might be the alternate. But I don't like it.' *Davis*

7 'I'm helping Piper out emotionally. Am I turning into Michelle? Have I been doing hair flips?' *Emily*

8 'I'd much rather be dancing with Henry than fighting with him.' *Summer*

JACQUIE

SUMMER

DAVIS

KENZIE

AMY

EMILY

PIPER

OZZY

ANSWERS: 1-OZZY, 2-PIPER, 3-JACQUIE, 4-SUMMER 5-KENZIE, 6-DAVIS, 7-EMILY, 8-AMY

PLAN THE NEXT STEP'S SHOW!

USE THIS BULLET JOURNAL TO WRITE DOWN EVERYTHING YOU NEED TO DO.

DANCERS

Which dancers will perform which dances?

- ☑ Soloist: Jaquie
- ☑ Music: stand up

- ☑ Duet: kingston + Lola
- ☑ Music: When the war is over

- ☑ Hip-hop routine: Henry
- ☑ Music: walking the dinosaur

- ☑ Contemporary routine: Noha + Jaquie
- ☑ Music: Fire

COSTUMES

Sketch out your ideas for the team's costumes.

COMPETITION DAY CHECKLIST

Schedule — write down what you and the team need to do before the big day.

Two weeks before:
- ● practise
- ● extra rehersals
- ○

One week before:
- ● Chill a bit
- ● normal rehersals - no extra
- ● Practise

One day before:
- ● practise - non stop
- ● leave studio
- ○

The day of the show:
- ● Calm every-ones nevers
- ● Mark through routine
- ● have a great time but also give it your all

The three things I am looking forward to the most:

1. Seeing the dancers give it 110.%

2. Me dancing

3. Doing the routines

PART one

NOAH'S DILEMMA

For a team to do well in competitions they need talent, strength, determination and … friendship! So when A-Troupe were told they had to choose between friendship and what was best for the team, it was always going to be a tough decision.

It's Dytto workshop day at the studios. Everyone is so hyped to be learning from one of the coolest hip-hop dancers around.

Everyone is having such a great time working with Dytto, that it seems they have forgotten one little thing – Noah's birthday.

Not even Jacquie has time to speak to Noah until they grab a smoothie at the end of the day.

As soon as they sit down, Jacquie squeals that she's had the best day ever. Noah doesn't seem excited at all. Jacquie asks him what's wrong – Noah isn't usually the type of guy to be sad. Noah explains that today is his birthday.

Jacquie starts apologising to Noah. He tells her not to worry, but he can't help feeling disappointed that even Jacquie has forgotten his birthday.

Then Jacquie jumps up from the bench they are sitting at. She unzips her jacket to reveal Noah's face on her T-shirt. She's planned him a surprise birthday party!

Noah is stunned. The Next Step dancers fill the café, all wearing matching T-shirts. Richelle produces a cake and the team clap and sing.

At that moment, Emily appears at Noah's shoulder. She looks at the cake and asks Noah if it is his birthday. Noah nods. Even though it is right there in bright red icing for everyone to read, Emily asks Noah if he is 18. When Noah says yes, Emily looks worried. Then she leaves.

It's odd, but Noah isn't going to let that stop him having the best night ever.

A few days later, Noah is called into Emily and Michelle's office. The two Studio Heads are usually full of energy, so seeing them look so worried gives Noah a feeling of dread in the pit of his stomach. Michelle begins telling Noah what an amazing dancer he is.

But straight-talking Emily interrupts her, explaining that because Noah is 18, the team will have to dance in the Senior Advanced Division at Regionals.

Will Noah stay and risk his team losing at Regionals, or will he leave The Next Step?

To be continued …

THE PERFECT DUET

To dance the perfect duet you have to be completely in sync with your partner. Who would be your ideal match?

1 It's time to work on choreography. Where do you start?

a. You come up with some suggestions but listen to your partner's suggestions, too

b. You just start dancing, have some fun and see what happens

c. You've got a clear idea in your head of the whole routine and can't wait to show your partner ✓

2 What would you say is your worst habit?

a. You can be a bit of a daydreamer

b. You joke around too much

c. You can be too much of a perfectionist

3 When do you like to rehearse?

a. In the mornings, when you are fresh. Then you have the rest of the day to do something fun with your friends

b. After lunch. You've got to be well fed to rehearse!

c. Anytime you can. The more rehearsals, the better the dance will be

4 What do you like to do when you aren't rehearsing or dancing?

a. Reading, drawing, or anything creative

b. Chilling out with your friends

c. Watching a dance show or shopping for dance supplies

5 What's the best thing about a duet partnership?

a. You get to know the other dancer really well. A connection with a friend really shows in your dancing, too!

b. Working with someone else means twice as much opportunity for jokes and fun!

c. You can do moves you can't do on your own – so the dance looks even better! ✓

6 What is the worst thing your duet partner could do?

a. Be mean about your dancing ✓

b. Be boring

c. Get the routine wrong

7 If you could hang out with anyone at The Next Step who would it be?

a. Henry

b. Piper ✓

c. Whoever the best dancer is!

8 What would be your perfect costume?

a. Something pretty and comfortable

b. A street or hip-hop themed outfit

c. Something high-end with lots of make-up to match

9 What would you say is your best quality?

a. I try to be as friendly as I can be, and I like to help others

b. I make people laugh, and I'm very chilled ✓

c. My dancing, obviously!

SUMMER

MOSTLY As

Just like Summer, you are kind and friendly, but you always work hard. You love spending time with your friends and you are always up for making more friends, too. You and Summer would create a happy, smiley and elegant dance together.

10 **What are your pre-show rituals?**

a. A big hug and a pep talk

b. A secret handshake and chest bumps

c. Deep breaths to get me in the zone

11 **What would you do if you fell out with your duet partner?**

a. Feel terrible and ask them to talk it through

b. Make a joke about it and try to forget that it happened

c. Try to find a new duet partner

12 **How would you feel if your duet partner made a mistake on stage?**

a. You would be worried about them

b. You would try to make the mistake part of the routine

c. You would dance extra hard to cover it up

FINN

MOSTLY Bs

It's fair to say you like to have fun – both in life and while dancing. Like Finn, you don't take yourself too seriously, but when it comes to dance you work hard to produce your best steps. You and Finn would create a light, fresh and upbeat dance.

MOSTLY Cs

Dance is important to you and you like to take it seriously. You know how you like things to be done and prefer to take the lead. You and Richelle may clash at first, but when you've worked things out, your dance would be perfection.

RICHELLE

CONTEMPORARY

IT'S ONE OF A-TROUPE'S MOST LOVED DANCE STYLES, BUT WHAT EXACTLY IS CONTEMPORARY?

#a dancer

WHAT IS IT?

Despite being called 'contemporary' this dance style was actually developed around 60 years ago. It is a mixture of modern dance, ballet and jazz.

Contemporary dancers use fluid, unstructured moves to create their dances and generally dance in bare feet, so they can really feel and connect with the floor.

WHAT'S TRICKY?

Maintaining the 'fluid' movement can be hard. Being 'fluid' means that your movements continue flowing through your body, almost like a wave.

TOP TIP!

When turning, pick a spot on the wall to focus on before and after each rotation. This will stop you getting too dizzy!

WHAT'S SO GREAT?

Contemporary dance can be danced to virtually any type of music because it is so adaptable.

TOP CONTEMPORARY TIPS

1 Get to know other dances. Any techniques you learn can be incorporated into contemporary dance.

2 Really listen to the music you are dancing to. How does it make you feel? Contemporary dance is about showing your feelings through dance.

3 Don't be sloppy. Although contemporary dance is fluid, if you don't think about each move, and finish it off correctly, your dance could look messy.

TOP MOVES

CHAINES TURN

This ballet move is often used to add elegance to a contemporary routine. Stand on your tiptoes with your arms in front of you as though you are hugging a large beach ball. Step to the right, placing most of your weight on your right foot. Spin on your right foot to face the back of the room. Then transfer your weight onto your left foot and spin on your left to face the front of the room. This is one turn.

LEAP

A leap adds dramatic flair to your contemporary routine. This could take the form of a grand jeté (a ballet term for a running jump, where your legs are stretched out into a split and your arms are rasied high in the air, usually above your head).

LUNGES

Lunges are sometimes used in contemporary dance to create a moment of stillness before stepping into a new move. A lunge is simply bending one leg in front of you, while the other leg remains straight behind. From there you can move into a leap or a spin, or raise your back leg up to create a beautiful shape.

DANCE LEGENDS

GET INSPIRED BY THESE STORIES OF WORLD-FAMOUS DANCERS.

MISTY COPELAND

Misty started her dance training at the age of 13. She was destined to be something special, as after only three months of dance classes she could dance *en pointe*. She was soon dancing professionally. Misty gained scholarships to prestigious ballet schools and eventually, in 2015, she was named principle dancer for the American Ballet Theatre – the first African American dancer to be given the role.

MARTHA GRAHAM

Martha was born in 1894 and studied ballet at one of the top schools in the world. However, Martha knew she wanted to do something different. She soon broke away from ballet to create her own style, which was more free and fluid. Martha is often referred to as the 'Mother of Modern Dance', as her dancing paved the way for Modern Dance to be recognised as a dance form. Martha set up her own company in 1926 and continued to dance until she was in her 70s.

FRED ASTAIRE

Fred Astaire is one of the dance world's most famous names. He starred in many films in the 1930s and 40s and is best known for his light-footed dance style that made even complicated routines look easy. He became even more well known when he partnered with Ginger Rogers and created routines that blended the styles of ballroom, tap and even ballet.

BEYONCÉ

Beyoncé started dancing at the age of eight. Despite becoming famous for her musical ability, dancing has always been part of what makes her a superstar. The video for Beyoncé's hit *Single Ladies* has become iconic for its mix of vintage Fosse moves with modern J-Setting. It has been viewed online more than 700 million times.

MIKHAIL BARYSHNIKOV

Mikhail Baryshnikov became the most famous ballet dancer in the Soviet Union in the 1960s. In 1974 he moved to Canada and then to the US, performing across the country. His precision, style and passion for ballet made him one of the most popular dancers in the world. After retiring from professional ballet, he became the artistic director of the American Ballet Theatre and went on to form his own dance company as well as acting on stage and screen.

ANNA PAVLOVA

Anna Pavlova was born in 1881, in Russia. She studied at the Imperial Ballet School, and was so talented that she made her company debut in 1899, at just 18 years old. She soon became their prima ballerina. Pavlova was best known for performing the title role in *The Dying Swan*. In 1911 she formed her own ballet company, which became the first ballet company to tour the world!

DID YOU KNOW?

The famous meringue, fresh fruit and cream dessert, Pavlova, was named after Anna Pavlova!

19

HERE'S HENRY!

HE HAS A BIG SMILE AND A BIG HEART TO MATCH!

Henry is usually a calm, happy member of The Next Step. When he first arrived at the studio, however, he had to deal with drama from his ex-girlfriend Jacquie. After some ups and downs, the pair found a way to be happy for each other.

His friends often tease him that he falls in love too easily, but he seems to have finally found his perfect match with Summer! He's a brilliant hip-hop dancer and everyone enjoys being around him.

DID YOU KNOW?

★ Henry missed his prom, so Amy held one at The Next Step for him!

★ He has two goldfish called Gerald and Jimmy.

FRIENDS

HENRY is best friends with NOAH, who shares his love of hip-hop. He also loves hanging out with his girlfriend, SUMMER.

FACT FILE

EYE COLOUR: Brown

HAIR COLOUR: Dark brown

MOST LIKELY TO: Fall in love (and talk about it!)

LEAST LIKELY TO: Have a diva tantrum

FAVOURITE DANCE STYLE: Hip-hop

SHE IS DRIVEN, TALENTED AND FOCUSED. SHE WILL DO ANYTHING TO TAKE THE NEXT STEP TO THE TOP.

Richelle has been at The Next Step since J-Troupe, but even as a young dancer Richelle was ambitious. Richelle tried to break into A-Troupe long before any of the other dancers her age, and was keen to be Dance Captain as soon as possible.

Although she might come across as tough, Richelle has had her heart broken by fellow high-flyer Elliot, who dumped her to pursue his own dance dreams. She is super loyal to The Next Step and would do anything to help them win.

FACT FILE

EYE COLOUR: Green

HAIR COLOUR: Blonde

MOST LIKELY TO: Take the lead

LEAST LIKELY TO: Be happy in the back row

FAVOURITE DANCE STYLE: Acro and ballet

DID YOU KNOW?

Even when Richelle was in J-Troupe Emily could see her potential, and she coached her for a while.

She once had a crush on Noah – but she's totally over it now.

IT'S RICHELLE!

21

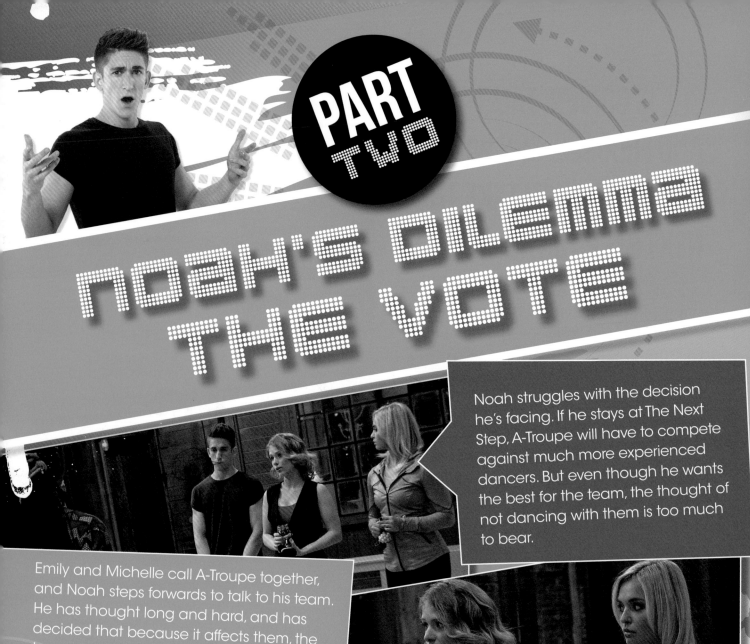

PART TWO

NOAH'S DILEMMA
THE VOTE

Noah struggles with the decision he's facing. If he stays at The Next Step, A-Troupe will have to compete against much more experienced dancers. But even though he wants the best for the team, the thought of not dancing with them is too much to bear.

Emily and Michelle call A-Troupe together, and Noah steps forwards to talk to his team. He has thought long and hard, and has decided that because it affects them, the team should make the decision.

Michelle is holding two bags of marbles, one white, one red. The team will take part in a vote. If they think Noah should stay in the team, they should drop a white marble in the jar. If they think Noah should leave, they should drop in a red one.

A-Troupe is stunned. They are in danger of losing their best dancer … and their friend. Emily gives each dancer a red marble and a white marble, and asks them to secretly drop their choice into the jar. Immediately, A-Troupe start arguing about the best thing to do.

The time has come to vote. No matter what anyone has said, each dancer has to make their own decision about whether Noah should leave or stay.

After the votes have been cast, Michelle slowly lifts the jar out of its pouch. There is one red marble among the many white ones. One dancer thinks Noah should leave. So that is it. Noah won't perform at Regionals.

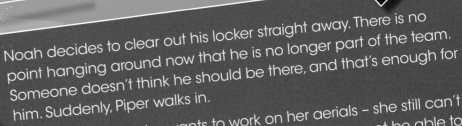

Noah decides to clear out his locker straight away. There is no point hanging around now that he is no longer part of the team. Someone doesn't think he should be there, and that's enough for him. Suddenly, Piper walks in.

She explains that she wants to work on her aerials – she still can't get them right. Noah says he will help her. He may not be able to help the team win Regionals, but he can still help a friend work on her technique.

The practise is going well, but Piper seems upset. Finally, she turns to Noah. She admits that she voted for him to leave. Noah is hurt, as Piper is one of his oldest friends, but he doesn't blame her. Piper is suddenly filled with regret, doubting her decision.

The next morning, the atmosphere in Studio A is flat. No one can believe that Noah has gone. Then, Emily and Michelle march out of their office with some important news.

Michelle announces that the team will be competing in the Senior Advanced Division at Regionals. Everyone is confused. It doesn't make sense! Then … Noah walks in. Emily explains that they will be competing at the senior level, because Noah is returning to The Next Step!

Noah jogs into the studio and is greeted by a giant group hug. He catches Piper's eye and smiles. Last night, Piper called Emily and Michelle and told them that she had changed her mind. The competition is going to be tough, but as a team these guys can do anything, right?

To be continued …

HAIR on POINTE

TRAINING: FISHTAIL BRAID

When you are running drills, working on your strength, or figuring out a new move, the last thing you want to be doing is fixing your hair every five minutes. Braids are a perfect way to keep your hair neat, tidy and out of your face, and a fishtail braid is a cute update on the classic style.

1. Put your hair in a ponytail. Then divide it into two even sections.

2. Take a thin section of hair from the outside of the left section and pass it over to the right section.

3. Pull a thin section of hair from the outside of the right section and pass it over to the left section.

4. Continue repeating steps 2 and 3. Try not to be too neat with your sections as this will add to the overall look.

5. When all of your hair is braided, secure it at the bottom with a hair tie.

6. Gently pull and flatten the braid to enhance the look.

You will need:
A HAIRBRUSH
HAIR TIES

24

REHEARSALS: MINI BUNS

You will need:
**A HAIRBRUSH
HAIR TIES
HAIR PINS**

When you are in rehearsals you need a style that keeps your hair up out of your way, and that can be restyled at a moment's notice. These mini buns work perfectly, and they are super cute, too.

1 Split your hair with a centre parting, and brush into two neat sections.

2 Take the first section and collect it as though you are going to make a ponytail.

3 Secure with a hair tie, but only pull your hair halfway through on the last wind round.

4 Fan out your hair to make it look more bun-like.

5 If you have very long hair, quickly wrap the ends around your mini-bun and secure with a hair pin.

6 Repeat on the other section.

TRY LEAVING THE BOTTOM HALF OF YOUR HAIR DOWN AND PUTTING TWO MINI BUNS TOWARDS THE TOP OF YOUR HEAD FOR A SLIGHTLY DIFFERENT LOOK.

SHOWTIME: BUN

You will need:
**A HAIRBRUSH
HAIR TIES
HAIR PINS
HAIRSPRAY**

For a serious dance show, a lot of dancers wear their hair in a sleek bun. Follow these steps to get a practical and professional-looking bun.

1. Brush your hair into a neat high ponytail.

2. Divide the ponytail into two sections, then start to twist one of the sections.

3. As you twist, begin to wrap the hair around your ponytail.

4. Pin your twist with wide hair pins to keep it in place.

5. Repeat steps 3 and 4 with the remaining section of hair, wrapping it in the same direction around your ponytail.

6. If your bun has hair sticking out, use a hair net over the top to create a super-neat effect. Secure it with another hair pin.

7. Finish everything off with some hairspray, to make sure that your hair stays in place while you perform.

25

HIP-HOP

HIP-HOP IS ONE OF THE STUDIO'S FAVOURITE DANCE STYLES. FIND OUT HOW THIS DANCE GOT SO POPULAR, AND TRY PERFORMING ONE OF ITS SIGNATURE MOVES!

WHAT IS IT?

Hip-hop dance developed from hip-hop music in 1970s New York. It includes a variety of styles, from breakdancing to 'popping and locking'. Ozzy, Kenzie, Henry and Finn all love hip-hop dance.

WHAT'S SO GREAT?

It's a lot of fun! Once you get the hang of some basic moves, you can use your imagination to come up with your own variations. It isn't as strict as ballet, so you can improvise and mix up steps in your hip-hop routine.

WHAT'S TRICKY?

Although hip-hop looks free-flowing, the moves need to hit the beat exactly to look right. They also take a lot of athleticism and involve some acro movements, too.

TOP HIP-HOP TIPS

 Relax. Hip-hop moves look better when your body isn't tense and you can bounce from one move to the next.

 Be comfortable. Most hip-hop dancers wear trainers and comfy clothes so that nothing restricts their movements.

3 Feel the music. The music is the start of everything in hip-hop. You need to know the change in beats and pace to make sure you hit your moves at the right time.

TOP TIP!
The Prep is a great start to any hip-hop routine.

TOP MOVES

THE PREP

The Prep is a classic hip-hop move that has four steps. It's called 'The Prep' because it mimics how you 'prepare' yourself before going out!

1 Start by getting the bounce. Throughout The Prep, you will do a double bounce on your left leg, before doing a double bounce on your right leg. Do this by bending your legs slightly and bobbing up and down in time with the music. Move your weight from one leg to the other after each double bounce. Keep repeating this move.

2 Step one is called 'check the mirror'. Bounce on your left leg, and twist your torso to the right. As you bounce, bring your palms up in front of your face, as though you are checking your reflection in them. Have one palm behind the other, then switch your hands round on the second bounce. Then return to face the front before the next move.

3 The second part is called 'brush your shoulder'. Bounce on your right leg, turning your face towards the left. Simply brush off your left shoulder twice with your right hand, in time with your bounce.

4 The third part is called 'wipe your clothes'. Go back to bouncing on your left leg. Pick up your right leg and, using both hands, brush your thigh twice, as if you were brushing off dirt.

5 The final part of the dance is called 'check your hair'. Bounce on your right leg, turning your body towards the left. Smooth either side of your head with one hand after the other, in time with the bounce.

FIND YOUR PLACE ON THE TEAM!

Follow the flow to discover your true place at The Next Step Studio.

ARE YOU A DANCE CAPTAIN, STUDIO HEAD OR SOLOIST?

Would you rather be on stage or cheering from the sidelines?

CHEERING ON → Do you always do your homework on time?

YES

MOSTLY ...

SOMETIMES

Do your friends come to you for advice?

OF COURSE

ON STAGE

I LOVE IT!

YES

Are you great at coming up with new routines?

SOMETIMES → Do you like to be in charge of group projects?

I'D RATHER NO

Are you great at planning sleepovers?

DEFINITELY

STUDIO HEAD

It's a tough job being in charge, but you don't mind. You would work hard to make the studio a success – even if it means missing out on all the fun of dancing.

NOT REALLY

YES

DANCE CAPTAIN

Would you be okay with losing your spot in a show to a better dancer?

NO

You believe in yourself and have the confidence to lead others, too. You would make a great Dance Captain as you are firm but fair, and you look out for your friends.

NO

It's showtime. Are you nervous?

YES

SOLOIST

SERIOUS

You love performing, whether it's in a group, a duet, or by yourself. You're so passionate about dance that you're the perfect choice for Soloist.

Is rehearsing fun, or really serious?

FUN

IT'S OZZY!

HE MIGHT ACT THE FOOL, BUT OZZY IS ONE OF THE SWEETEST MEMBERS OF A-TROUPE.

Ozzy is a sweet, optimistic member of the studio. He tries his best and never stops going after the things he wants. After leaving J-Troupe, he tried hard to get into A-Troupe, and eventually found his spot among the team.

He's a loyal friend, and tries to help everyone out – even when his 'help' come across as interfering. He was convinced that he and Richelle were meant to be together, it just took Richelle a while to see that Ozzy is WAY better for her than her creepy ex-boyfriend Elliot was.

FRIENDS

KINGSTON is his best friend and everyone at The Next Step thinks he is a sweetheart. **FINN** and **HENRY** are some of his closest friends.

DID YOU KNOW?

★ Ozzy is a real prankster. He once convinced Henry, Kingston, Amy and Le Troy that there was a country called Litvania. There isn't. He also declared that the national dance of Lithuania involved walking like an ostrich. It doesn't.

★ He'd love to be a video game designer – if he wasn't a dancer, of course!

FACT FILE

EYE COLOUR: Brown

HAIR COLOUR: Brown

MOST LIKELY TO: Make you laugh

LEAST LIKELY TO: Tell a lie

FAVOURITE DANCE STYLE: Hip-hop

LET'S HEAR IT FOR A-TROUPE'S FEISTIEST HIP-HOP STAR.

When Kenzie joined The Next Step she was part of Miss Angela's new crew. However, Kenzie soon let the rest of A-Troupe know whose side she was on, and helped to get rid of Miss Angela when things turned sour.

Kenzie is super confident and doesn't mind telling you how great she is. The truth is, she is pretty great! She's also a loyal friend and is the perfect person to have on your side in an argument. (You certainly don't want to be on the opposite side!)

EYE COLOUR: Brown

HAIR COLOUR: Black

MOST LIKELY TO: Tell you how good she is

LEAST LIKELY TO: Go behind your back

FAVOURITE DANCE STYLE: Hip-hop and acro

DID YOU KNOW?

★ Kenzie's dad used to own a diner.

★ She can speak French. C'est magnifique!

FRIENDS

KENZIE became good friends with **DAVIS** (Jacquie's little sister) after helping her practise for a spot in the Regional's hip-hop routine.

CUE KENZIE!

YOU'RE THE STAR!

THE NEXT STEP HAS JUST FOUND ITS NEWEST MEMBER. BUT WHO ARE THEY? WHAT'S GOING TO HAPPEN? WILL THEY BE A STAR AT REGIONALS OR LEAVE FOR ANOTHER STUDIO? IT IS TIME TO FIND OUT ...

FOLLOW THE CHARTS TO CREATE YOUR NEXT STEP CHARACTER NAME.

SAY MY NAME!

1

BIRTHDAY MONTH	FIRST NAME
JANUARY	STAR
FEBRUARY	PHILLY
MARCH	FLIPZ
APRIL	DAZZLE
MAY	SPARKS
JUNE	JAZZ
JULY	AJ
AUGUST	FABZ
SEPTEMBER	ALI
OCTOBER	JAY-JAY
NOVEMBER	HEART
DECEMBER	XANNA

2

EYE COLOUR	LAST NAME
BLUE	RAMIREZ
BROWN	GROVER
GREEN	HAWKINS
HAZEL	LOWTHER
GREY	DE SILVA

3

HAIR COLOUR	DANCE SPECIALITY
BLONDE	BALLET
DARK BLONDE	ACRO
BROWN	HIP-HOP
BLACK	CONTEMPORARY
RED	JAZZ

ROLL WITH IT

ROLL THE DICE THREE TIMES TO SEE WHAT HAPPENS TO YOUR CHARACTER IN THE NEXT SERIES OF THE NEXT STEP.

1

⚀ You audition for **A-TROUPE** and give an incredible performance. Everyone loves you at first, then …

⚁ You're the star of A-Troupe and sure to become **DANCE CAPTAIN** this year, but there's a new dancer who swoops in to take it off you.

⚂ You audition for **B-TROUPE**, but you are so good that you get a spot on **A-TROUPE**!

⚃ You want to audition for A-Troupe. **EMILY** and **MICHELLE** think you are a spy, but then …

⚄ You accidentally knock into another dancer at the **A-TROUPE** audition and hurt their leg. You get in, but they don't.

⚅ You forget your water, so **OZZY** runs out and gets you a new bottle. You suspect he has a bit of a crush on you, but forget about it when you find out you've made it onto A-Troupe!

2

⚀ You get the solo at **REGIONALS**, but Richelle is upset that someone new has been given the spot.

⚁ **SUMMER** injures herself at Regionals and you step up to take her solo spot.

⚂ You get an attack of the **NERVES** at Regionals and the troupe rally around to look after you.

⚃ **HENRY** sees a flyer for a rival dance group in your bag. You explain that you're not going anywhere.

⚄ Your duet with **NOAH** goes really well at Regionals and everyone is sure The Next Step are going to win.

⚅ You help **KENZIE** when she stumbles in the group dance at Regionals. Together, you make it look like part of the dance.

3

⚀ The Next Step **WIN REGIONALS!** Everyone agrees they couldn't have done it without you.

⚁ The Next Step **LOSE REGIONALS**, but everyone believes they tried their hardest and they can't wait to try again next year.

⚂ The Next Step **WIN REGIONALS!** You've loved your time at The Next Step … but another studio has caught your eye.

⚃ The Next Step **LOSE REGIONALS!** But at the after-party an agent offers to sign you up to do a world tour. What will you do?

⚄ The Next Step **WIN REGIONALS!** Emily and Michelle ask you to coach B-Troupe next year, but you want to stay with A-Troupe.

⚅ The Next Step **LOSE REGIONALS!** You feel like it's all your fault, but Piper cheers you up with a round of smoothies at Shakes and Ladders.

ENERGISING SMOOTHIES

Add a handful of chia seeds to your smoothie to give you an extra burst of goodness!

THE PERFECT DRINK FOR BUSY REHEARSALS, A BREAK DURING TRAINING OR JUST CHILLING WITH YOUR FRIENDS.

Pass your smoothie through a sieve to get rid of any lumps.

Use almond, coconut, oat or soya milk if you don't want to use dairy.

BERRY BLITZ

- 700g frozen summer fruits
- 1 banana
- 300ml milk or yoghurt

1. **CHOP** the banana into small pieces and **ADD** to a blender.
2. **ADD** the frozen summer fruits to the blender.
3. Finally, **POUR** in your yogurt or milk.
4. **BLEND** until there are no lumps of banana left.

TALL GLASSES WITH PAPER STRAWS ARE THE BEST WAY TO SERVE YOUR SMOOTHIES! OR, POP THEM IN A TRAVEL CUP AND DRINK THEM ON THE GO.

THE GREEN ONE

- 130g spinach or kale
- 130ml water
- 130g pineapple or mango (or a mix!). Frozen is better.

1. Put the spinach and water into a blender and **BLEND** until smooth.
2. **ADD** in your frozen fruit and **BLEND** again until there are no lumps remaining.
3. **TASTE** your smoothie to get the balance of spinach and fruit just right (add more fruit if the spinach is too overpowering).

COCONUT CREAM

- 400ml coconut milk
- 4 bananas
- 2 tbsp honey
- Handful of ice cubes
- Shaved coconut, to garnish

1. **CHOP** the bananas into small pieces.
2. **ADD** the chopped banana, milk and honey to a blender and **BLEND** until smooth.
3. **ADD** the ice cubes and **BLEND** again.
4. **POUR** into glasses and top with a sprinkling of shaved coconut.

If you use almond milk, make sure to check if anyone is allergic to nuts before serving.

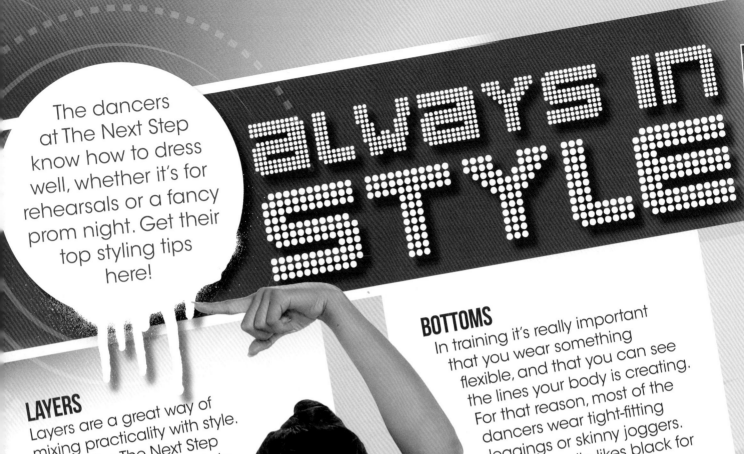

The dancers at The Next Step know how to dress well, whether it's for rehearsals or a fancy prom night. Get their top styling tips here!

LAYERS

Layers are a great way of mixing practicality with style. Most of the The Next Step girls wear colourful vests to keep their core warm, with another vest or T-shirt over the top. Summer shows off her girly side with florals, while Kenzie likes bold designs and mesh panels.

BOTTOMS

In training it's really important that you wear something flexible, and that you can see the lines your body is creating. For that reason, most of the dancers wear tight-fitting leggings or skinny joggers. While Richelle likes black for showing off those dancing lines, Davis mixes it up with mesh panelling and Summer goes for brighter colours.

GUY STYLE

The boys like to show off their personalities, even in training. While Finn and Noah go for simple, preppy T-shirts, Henry likes to layer and Ozzy shows off his quirky side with tie-dye T-shirts.

PROM QUEENS

WHEN AMY THREW A PROM FOR HENRY, IT GAVE THE DANCERS A CHANCE TO SHOW OFF THEIR STYLE OUTSIDE OF TRAINING.

AMY

Amy's dress showed off her fun, happy side, with a sweet floral print and glittering gems. The full skirt was perfect for dancing at the prom!

HENRY AND SUMMER

Henry and Summer made a stunning couple at the prom. Her dreamy dress, with layers of chiffon, worked perfectly with Henry's vintage-inspired suit and hat combo.

PIPER

Piper is a bit of a tomboy and didn't fancy going full-on girly for the prom. Instead she chose a suit jacket, red bow tie and cute cut-off trousers. A true style statement!

DOUBLE TROUBLE

When Richelle and Jacquie ended up in the same dress at prom, they fell out at first – then they decided to customise! Richelle chose to give her dress a harder edge with black ribbon and diamanté, while Jacquie went for bold florals. It just goes to show that when you are a team, you can get through anything!

ALL HAIL KINGSTON

THIS BOY WON'T LET ANYTHING STOP HIM FROM UPPING HIS GAME!

Kingston is a self-taught dancer and actually became semi-famous for uploading videos of himself to the internet. He's always felt a little insecure about his lack of professional training, but that just makes him work harder, and he's learning all the time.

He and Ozzy make a great team, helping each other out where they can. Ozzy helped Kingston to get his grades back up in school, making sure he could study and stay in The Next Step.

FRIENDS

Despite joining The Next Step when the studio was split into TNS East and TNS West, **KINGSTON** managed to make some great friends, including his best pal, **OZZY.**

FACT FILE

EYE COLOUR: Dark brown

HAIR COLOUR: Black

MOST LIKELY TO: Put in some extra hours after training

LEAST LIKELY TO: Let anything get in his way

FAVOURITE DANCE STYLE: Hip-hop

DID YOU KNOW?

★ Kingston once attended Baby Ballet classes (when he most definitely wasn't a baby!) to improve his technique.

★ He bites his nails when he is nervous.

38

SHE IS DETERMINED, FIERCE AND DEFINITELY NOT ONE TO SIT ON THE SIDELINES.

Jacquie always had her sights set on joining A-Troupe, so when she finally got a spot, she was going to make sure she kept it! She's a determined dancer and would do anything for The Next Step, so when emotional family drama get in the way, her reaction is to fight first, think later.

Jacquie has had to deal with her ex-boyfriend (Henry) and her little sister (Davis) turning up and joining A-Troupe, too, but she always found comfort with her boyfriend Noah. It seemed as though nothing was going to tear these two apart, until Noah turned 18 …

DID YOU KNOW?

★ As well as dancing, Jacquie is a bit of a chemistry whizz. She helped Kingston with his chemistry homework using an egg dipped in vinegar.

★ Jacquie's sister Davis joined A-Troupe for a while and got nicknamed 'Blonde Jacquie'.

FACT FILE

EYE COLOUR: Hazel

HAIR COLOUR: Dark brown

MOST LIKELY TO: Compete as hard as she can

LEAST LIKELY TO: Give up her spot on the team

FAVOURITE DANCE STYLE: Acro and contemporary

FRIENDS

RICHELLE and JACQUIE are competitive but have developed a strong friendship and always have each other's backs.

HEY, JACQUIE!

PART THREE

NOAH'S DILEMMA THE PLAY

With Noah firmly back on the team, it's time to start focusing on Regionals … and the three dances that are going to win them the title. Hip-hop, contemporary and ballet. Noah and Richelle are joined by Chloe in Studio A to work on their choreography.

It is clear Chloe is impressed by Noah. She pulls him to one side and tells him that he could make the leap to pro. She hands him a business card and tells him that there is an audition coming up for Robin Hood, the Musical. Chloe thinks that Noah should go for it.

Noah stares at the card. A musical would be a chance for him to shine on his own.

But, if he goes to the audition and gets the part, he will have to leave The Next Step straight after Regionals – and that means leaving Jacquie, too. All day Noah thinks about what he should do.

Jacquie walks into the studio. She calmly tells him that Richelle told her about the audition. Noah says he doesn't know what to do. The production goes on tour all around the world, so they wouldn't be able see each other.

Hiding how scared she really feels, Jacquie tells Noah that he should stop stalling and make the call. This is such a big opportunity – he shouldn't pass it up.

The next day, Noah is in the bright hallways of a musical theatre casting agency. He is due to go to A-Troupe rehearsals soon, but this audition is too good an opportunity to miss. Noah takes a seat and tries to focus.

Elliot walks into the room and spots Noah. He spends the next 20 minutes trying to get into Noah's head – telling him that, honestly, the part is already Elliot's. Finally, Noah gets called into the audition.

When he comes out, Noah is faced with an angry Emily. She says that Noah should have been at rehearsals hours ago. The two of them head back to the studio together.

Back at the studio, Michelle agrees to go over everything Noah has missed step-by-step. But Noah has already seen a video of the routine and knows it inside out. He performs the dance – it is perfect. Michelle realises that there isn't anything she can teach Noah anymore.

Noah and Michelle decide to grab a drink in Shakes and Ladders after practice. When they arrive, a phone rings across the café. Suddenly, they see Elliot jumping for joy – he's got the role in Robin Hood.

Noah puts his head in his hands, but Michelle tells him how amazing he is. She thinks that he should consider leaving The Next Step. The part in Robin Hood isn't meant to be, but there will be other opportunities ahead. All he has to do is reach out and take them.

To be continued...

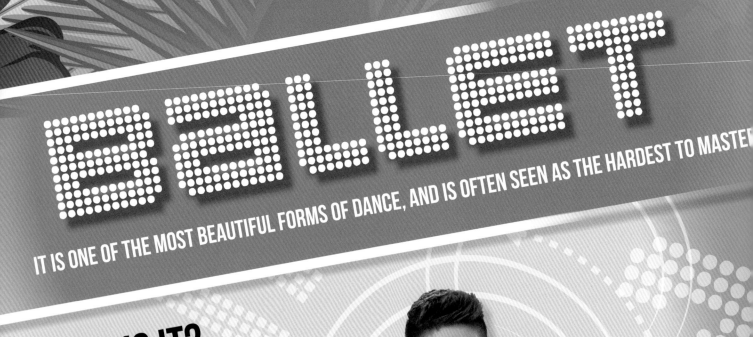

BALLET

IT IS ONE OF THE MOST BEAUTIFUL FORMS OF DANCE, AND IS OFTEN SEEN AS THE HARDEST TO MASTER

WHAT IS IT?

Ballet became popular in the 17th century. It is a beautiful style of dance and it takes years to master the techniques needed to dance it professionally. Most ballets revolve around a story, with the most famous being Swan Lake, The Nutcracker, Giselle and Sleeping Beauty.

WHAT'S SO GREAT?

Ballet is arguably the most graceful and beautiful form of dance. It has lent its style to contemporary, modern and even some acro and hip-hop moves. If you know the basics of ballet, you can apply it to almost any dance.

WHAT'S TRICKY?

Ballet dancers often dance *en pointe*, which means they stand on the very tips of their toes, in special pointe shoes.

TOP BALLET TIPS

1 Stretch. A lot of ballet dancers like to do yoga and Pilates, as stretching helps them to reach further in positions and keep their core strong.

2 Practise. The more times you do a move, the more it stays in your memory. The moves will eventually become second nature to you, like tying your shoelaces.

3 Don't be afraid to make mistakes. The only way ballet dancers learn to do the moves right is by getting them wrong many, many times first! With practise you will improve.

TOP TIP!
Ballet dancers talk about keeping their 'core' strong. Your 'core' is a set of muscles in the middle of your body.

TOP MOVES

FIRST ARABESQUE

1 Start by standing in First Position (with your heels pressed together and your toes pointed outwards to make a V shape).

2 Slide your right foot along the floor to point to the back of the room, leaving your left leg where it is. Raise your arms into a soft shape, with your right arm stretched out to the right, and your left arm stretching forward.

3 Carefully lift your right leg off the ground, keeping your toes pointed and both legs stretched out straight. Try to hold this position for a few seconds before lowering your right leg.

SAUTÉ

1 Start by standing in First Position (with your heels pressed together and your toes pointed outwards to make a V shape). Hold your arms down in front of you, bending your elbows slightly and bringing your fingertips towards each other, but do not let them touch. Your arms should make a low circle.

2 Bend your knees slightly. Then push your feet off the ground and jump into the air.

3 As you jump, straighten your legs and point your toes. Your legs should come apart slightly, so that they make an upside down V shape.

4 Try to land softly, back in First Position, with your heels together and toes pointed outwards.

ENERGY BITES

Three simple recipes to make healthy and delicious snacks on the go!

PEANUT BUTTER BALLS

- 100g pecans or ground almonds
- 75g raisins
- 1 tbsp cocoa powder
- 1 tbsp honey
- 50g shaved coconut
- 2 tbsp peanut butter

1. If you are using pecans, **CHOP** them finely or pop them in a food processor to break them up.

2. **MIX** everything together in a large bowl until it starts to form a dough.

3. Separate the dough into portions and use the flats of your palms to **ROLL** it into ping-pong-sized balls.

4. **POP** the balls on a baking tray in the fridge for around 15 minutes, to firm up.

Some people are very allergic to nuts. Make sure you check before handing any home-made goodies out to friends!

FRUITY SQUARES

- 130g rolled oats
- 3 ripe bananas (mashed)
- 130g dried apricots (chopped)
- 5 tbsp olive oil or melted coconut oil
- 2 tbsp shaved coconut
- 2 tbsp ground flaxseed or chia seeds

1. Put all the ingredients into a large bowl and **STIR**. You might need to use your hands for this! **MIX** until it becomes a sticky dough.

2. **LINE** a square or rectangular cake tin with baking paper and **TIP** the dough in.

3. **PRESS** the mixture down until it reaches the corners of the tin and is more or less flat on top.

4. **PLACE** in the freezer for around 15 minutes.

5. When the mixture is firm, **CUT** it into bite-sized squares.

THESE ONES ARE GLUTEN AND DAIRY-FREE.

'THESE ARE MY FAVOURITE!'

CHOCOLATE CHIP AND HONEY BITES

- 400ml coconut milk
- 180g rolled oats
- 2 tbsp chia seeds
- 75g almond or peanut butter
- 70g honey or maple syrup
- 1 tsp vanilla extract
- A pinch of salt
- 70g chocolate chips

1. Add all the ingredients, apart from the chocolate chips, to a large bowl or food processor. **MIX** together until they form a dough.

2. **STIR** through the chocolate chips until they are evenly distributed.

3. **SEPARATE** the dough into portions and use the flats of your palms to **ROLL** it into ping-pong-sized balls.

4. **PLACE** the balls on a baking tray in the fridge for around 15-20 minutes.

WHAT'S YOUR DANCE DESTINY?

Do you dream of a future in dance?
Take the quiz to discover what you could be!

3 What's the best part of putting on a show?
a. Opening night
b. Watching it all come together
c. Hanging out with friends! ✔

4 What trait do you value the most?
a. Talent
b. Creativity ✔
c. Kindness

5 How would you cheer up a friend or sibling who was feeling down?
a. Tell them a joke
b. Have a film night with popcorn and chocolate ✔
c. Talk through why they are upset

6 How would you talk to a friend you haven't seen for a while?
a. Video chat
b. Message ✔
c. Going over to their house!

7 Imagine your friend was the lead in a dance show, but got sick on opening night. How would you help?
a. You would step in and take their part
b. You would see which of the cast was best to take their place
c. You would stay at home with them and make sure they were feeling okay

8 What are you most likely to wear?
a. A party dress
b. Sportswear
c. Anything comfy

1 It's time for the school play. What do you put your name down for?
a. Acting
b. Directing
c. Anything as long as you can take part ✔

2 You've been given a project to do for school. How do you present your work?
a. A dramatic performance
b. A scrapbook filled with pictures and writing ✔
c. A talk to the class with a question and answer session after

9 You have a mountain of homework to do, but you really want to go to dance practice. What do you do?

a. Go to dance practice, then stay up really late doing your homework

b. Ask your teacher for a few more days to finish your homework ✓

c. Do your homework and miss practice. There's always next week

10 Would you like to travel when you grow up?

a. Yes! I can't wait to explore ✓

b. If it's a part of my dream job

c. Maybe, but I don't mind if I don't

11 Your friends and family would describe you as:

a. Outgoing, creative and happy

b. Confident, thoughtful and energetic

c. Patient, kind and caring

12 Your best feature is:

a. Your star quality

b. Your organisation skills

c. Your kindness

WEST END STAR

MOSTLY As

Nothing but bright lights and the roar of a crowd will do for you! You love performing, and whether it's being part of the chorus or the lead role, you want to be on stage. It's hard work, but you're ready for it.

CHOREOGRAPHER

MOSTLY Bs

You would love to spend your future listening to music, putting routines together in your head and watching them come to life. You could work with bands, dance shows, or in the theatre.

TEACHER

MOSTLY Cs

Spending your days sharing your love of dance is your dream destiny. As a teacher you get to show the next generation of dancers just how great dance is. What could be better?

GO FINN!

HE'S THE GOOFY GUY WITH A BIG HEART AND SICK SKILLS ON THE DANCE FLOOR.

Finn joined The Next Step Dance Studio with Miss Angela, alongside Summer and Kenzie. He has a heart of gold and knew right away that his loyalties lay with the original Next Step dancers. He's funny, kind and has a bit of a soft spot for Piper.

Finn's incredible acro and hip-hop moves make him an essential member of the team. While his laid-back style means he's a voice of calm when things start to get dramatic in the studio.

FRIENDS

FINN soon found firm friends in **OZZY** and **KINGSTON,** as well as trying his hardest to show his best side to **PIPER.**

FACT FILE

EYE COLOUR: Blue

HAIR COLOUR: Light brown

MOST LIKELY TO: Say something funny

LEAST LIKELY TO: Be mean to anyone

FAVOURITE DANCE STYLE: Hip-hop and acro

DID YOU KNOW?

★ Finn is the tallest member of the studio at 6ft 2" (1.8 metres). He is a whole foot taller than Richelle!

★ He once starred in a TV advert for Fruity Moons breakfast cereal as a kid.

SHE'S THE ACRO QUEEN WITH HER SIGHTS SET ON STARDOM.

Amy has had a bumpy ride at The Next Step Dance Studio, but she has always known what she wants – to be the best dancer she can be. After finally making it onto A-Troupe, Amy constantly got passed over for spots in competitions. Finally, she decided that it was time to make a change and left the studio for a troupe that appreciates her talents.

Amy has a kind heart, which makes it easy for her to find friends. When Henry reveals that he missed his school prom, Amy decides to throw a prom at the studio for him. Even though things don't go exactly to plan, everyone ends up having a great time.

DID YOU KNOW?

Amy's mother was a professional dancer and really wants Amy to be a star, too.

Amy leaves The Next Step for Acro Nation. She becomes their lead dancer.

Amy once spilt her trousers while performing on stage. She had to perform the rest of the dance with her legs together to stop the tear from being seen by the audience.

HEY, AMY!

MAKE-UP MASTERCLASS

The best make-up looks for rehearsals, hanging with friends and showtime!

REHEARSALS

The Next Step dancers keep their faces fresh for rehearsals. When you are working your body hard you are likely to sweat, so having lots of make-up on is not the healthiest thing for your skin – make-up plus sweat equals clogged pores! **JACQUIE** and **AMY** keep it simple with clean faces and moisturiser. They use waterproof mascara and a touch of tinted lip balm, too.

- WASH YOUR FACE AND DAB SOME LIGHT MOISTURISER ON YOUR FACE AND NECK.

- PICK A NEUTRAL LIP BALM AND APPLY IT LIGHTLY TO YOUR LIPS.

- BRUSH THE TIPS OF YOUR EYELASHES WITH WATERPROOF MASCARA — NO NEED TO GO FROM ROOT TO TIP FOR REHEARSALS!

KEEP SOME HAND AND FOOT MOISTURISER IN YOUR KIT BAG TO LOOK AFTER THE MOST HARD-WORKING PARTS OF YOUR BODY!

TIME OUT

Even the most dedicated dancer has time out of the studio to have fun with their friends. **Richelle** upgrades her rehearsal look with pink lip gloss, a touch of eyeliner and some bronzer.

For Regionals, **Kenzie** and the rest of **The Next Step girls** wore dark lipstick and dark eyeshadow to contrast their simple outfits, and to make their expressions **pop** on stage.

Judges and audience members need to see how a dancer's face looks on stage, and for that they need a bit of stage make-up. A dancer's make-up also needs to compliment the dance they are doing.

- Use a sweep of liquid eyeliner across the top line of your eyelashes. If you don't feel confident about getting a straight line, ask a friend to do it for you.

- Always apply mascara after your liner. Start at the root of your lashes and sweep up to the tip.

- Prep your lips with some lip balm. Then outline your lips with a lipliner slightly darker than your lipstick colour – this will add definition to your lips and prevent smudges. Then, apply your chosen lipstick on top. Blot your lips with some tissue.

- Finally, dab some cream blush to the apples of your cheeks, to give you a healthy glow.

EYELINER AND MASCARA WILL HELP SHOW THE EXPRESSION IN YOUR EYES.

TOP TIP!

Look closely at your eyes. What colour are they? Do they have flecks of other colours in them? These are the colours that will look great as eyeshadow!

- Apply your bronzer first, adding a little to your forehead and cheekbones.

- Apply eyeliner by gently holding your eyelid down. Start at the point closest to your nose and draw a thin line, as close to your lashes as you can. Liquid liner works best, but you need a steady hand!

- Choose a light lip gloss or a neutral lipstick to finish your look. Blot away any excess lipstick with a paper towel.

DANCE DARES!

HOLD YOUR NERVE, SHOW OFF YOUR SKILLS AND WIN THE GAME!

HOW TO PLAY

This game works best with 2-4 players, but if there are more of you, you can separate into pairs or teams.

1 **CLEAR A SPACE TO PLAY** – you need a large area to dance in. Move any big pieces of furniture to the side, or even play outside.

2 **CUT OUT (OR COPY)** the cards on the opposite page. Shuffle the cards and place them face down, in a pile, to the side of your dance area.

3 Take it in turns to pick up a card and read out the 'DANCE DARE'.

4 The player must then decide to play or pass. If they pass, the dare gets passed on to the player on **THEIR LEFT.**

5 Whoever is taking the dare must then **PERFORM THE DARE.**

6 If the person who picked up the card completes the dare, they win the **POINTS.**

7 If the player has been passed the dare and they complete it, they win **DOUBLE THE POINTS.**

8 If the player has been **PASSED THE DARE** and they do not complete it, then the player who picked up the card gets the points.

9 Play until someone **REACHES 60 POINTS.** If you want the game to last longer, you can choose a higher score instead.

Task	Points
Name three famous dancers in 15 seconds.	15
Stand on one leg for 20 seconds without falling over.	15
Perform a pirouette.	10
Do the 'twist'.	10
Jump higher than the player on your right. ✓	15
Name four dance styles in 15 seconds.	10
Touch your toes without bending your knees.	10
Do a push-up.	10
Name five A-Troupe dancers in 15 seconds.	15
Choose and perform a dance style, see if the other players can guess which style it is.	10
Do an impression of Emily. ✓	15
Perform 'The Prep'.	10
Name three A-Troupe Dance Captains in 30 seconds. ✓	15
Compete with the other players to see who can do the highest kick. If you win, you get the points.	15
Do an impression of Miss Angela.	10
Do an impression of any of the A-Troupe dancers and see if another player can guess who it is.	15
Do a bridge.	10
Recreate a dramatic scene from a Next Step episode and see if the rest of the players recognise the scene.	15
Make up three couple names for any characters in The Next Step (e.g. Jackie and Noah become Janoah). ✓	15
Watch a dance from any episode of The Next Step and see if you can copy 10 seconds of it.	15
Spell 'The Next Step' backwards. ✓	10
Say an A-Troupe dancer's name backwards and see if the rest of the players can guess the name.	10
Name the A-Trouper you think is the cutest.	15
Name the A-Trouper who you think would make a great friend.	15
Do a Michelle-esque hair flip.	10
Review your last meal in the style of Emily reviewing a bad dance. E.g. 'That toast was completely burnt, I don't know why it bothered popping up!'.	15
Say which character you would like to: 1. Go to the cinema with, 2. Go on holiday with, and 3. Be stuck in a lift with.	15
Name the ex-The Next Step character you would most like to come back.	10
Floss for 20 seconds.	15
While blindfolded, draw a picture of Ozzy.	15
Recreate a funny scene from a Next Step episode and see if the rest of the players recognise the scene.	10

NAME YOUR TROUPE!

If you've ever dreamed about starting your own dance troupe but just couldn't think of the right name, then check out the chart below!

1 First, find your birth month, then read across to discover the first part of your dance troupe's name.

BIRTH MONTH	1ST NAME
JANUARY	ENERGY
FEBRUARY	ULTIMATE
MARCH	ELECTRIC
APRIL	FIERCE
MAY	SUPER
JUNE	SPARKLE
JULY	ACRO
AUGUST	HIP-HOP
SEPTEMBER	DIAMOND
OCTOBER	POWER
NOVEMBER	FABULOUS
DECEMBER	SICK

2 Next, find your eye colour on the chart, then scan across to discover the second part of your troupe's name.

EYE COLOUR	2ND NAME
BLUE	STARS
BROWN	STEPPERS
GREEN	NATION
HAZEL	ACADEMY
GREY	FORCE

3 So, if you were born in March and your eyes are blue, your troupe would be called: **ELECTRIC STARS!**

Design a logo for your dance troupe

Can you tell which of these dance troupe names are real, and which are made up?

CARTE BLANCHE ☐ HOT SHOTS ☑ RIVERDANCE ☐

SMOOTHIE DANCERS ☐ BY THE BOOK ☑ UPSIDE DOWN SMILE ☐

Answers: Carte Blance, Hot Shots and Riverdance are real dance troupes.

Dancing and me!

USE THIS BULLET JOURNAL TO WRITE DOWN EVERYTHING YOU NEED TO DO.

The dance I'm best at is: Modern + Hip-Hop

I want to practise this dance style more:
Ballet

The dancer I most admire is:
Richelle + ~~you~~ Jaquie

If I could dance anywhere in the world it would be:

America + disney land paris

Use this space to write about your future dancing plans. Do you want to be a world-famous choreographer or star in your own show? Or maybe you want to keep dancing just to stay fit and have fun ...

Use this space to choreograph a dance routine. Think about the steps you have learned in this book. Which ones do you want to use?

I want to go on a dance world TOUR!

My three favourite songs to dance to are:
1. Fire
2. coming home
3. Sucker

DID YOU KNOW?

DANCE EXISTS IN EVERY COUNTRY ON THE PLANET, AND HAS BEEN AROUND FOR THOUSANDS OF YEARS. TAKE A LOOK AT THE AMAZING WORLD OF DANCE!

The world's longest conga line had **119,986** people in it. This World Record hasn't been beaten in over 30 years!

Dancing is good for your mind, as well as your body. Dancing can relieve stress and make you feel happy, due to chemicals called **DOPAMINE & SEROTONIN** being released when you exercise.

The **TARANTELLA** is a dance from Italy that is supposed to mimic what happens to you when you are bitten by a **TARANTULA!**

The average ballet tutu uses **10 METRES** of netting!

80% of all professional ballet dancers have at least one major injury in their careers, and most retire in their 30s.

Cave drawings prove that people have been dancing for thousands of years!

Popular dances in the 1960s were given strange names. There was the **FRUG, THE HITCH HIKER** and the **MASHED POTATO!**

In Romania, police officers were given ballet lessons to help them manage traffic more gracefully!

Dancing is a great way to keep you fit and healthy. Performing in a three-hour ballet can be the same, physically, as running for **19 MILES (30KM).**

An environmentally-friendly dance floor, which powers its own lights, was created in 2008. **ENERGY** is produced from the pressure that is applied to the floor when people dance on it – the more dancing, the brighter the lights!

BALLERINAS can get through lots of pairs of shoes in just one show! Wardrobe departments must keep fresh pairs of shoes ready for when the old ones scuff and **WEAR OUT**.

In Michigan, US, in 1923, dancers were only allowed to dance in pairs if they didn't look into each other's eyes!

The Waltz has been danced in England for over **200 YEARS.**

In October 2010, Mauro Peruzzi broke the **WORLD RECORD** for the number of breakdance windmills performed in 30 seconds. Mauro managed to perform 50 – that's one every 0.6 seconds!

WHICH DANCE STYLE SUITS YOU BEST?

COULD YOU MASTER TRICKY BALLET STEPS, OR ARE YOU MORE SUITED TO HIP-HOP MOVES?
LET'S FIND OUT!

START

What's your favourite thing to do in your spare time (apart from dance)?

READ

Does homework have to be perfect?

YES

Do you like following the rules?

SOMETIMES

NOT ALWAYS

CHILLING WTH FRIENDS

MORNINGS

What's better: mornings or afternoons?

AFTERNOONS

Is faster music always better?

YES

Do you always train hard?

I TRY → # BALLET

You prefer elegant moves with long lines. You don't mind a bit of hard work and can be a bit of a perfectionist – which is perfect for ballet!

IF POSSIBLE!

NO

Do you tend to worry?

SOMETIMES

CONTEMPORARY

NOT ALWAYS ...

NOT REALLY

You're quite a laid-back person, so the free-flowing style of contemporary is perfect for you. You like to feel the music, rather than hit a set of pre-determined steps.

Trainers or bare feet?

BARE FEET

MOST OF THE TIME

TRAINERS

HIP-HOP

You've got tons of energy and love to keep life upbeat. Hip-hop is all about showing off your fabulous moves and your super-cool attitude.

Do you have loads of energy?

ALWAYS

SUPER SUMMER!

SHE'S THE KINDEST DANCER AT THE NEXT STEP AND WOULD DO ANYTHING FOR HER TEAMMATES.

Summer came to The Next Step Dance Studio with Kenzie and Finn when Miss Angela took over as Studio Head. She tried her best to fit in, but couldn't help standing out because of her incredible talent.

When A-Troupe joined together to get rid of Miss Angela, Summer stood by them, and they soon saw what a lovely person she was. The troupe knew that Summer was a fabulous asset to the team and could help them go all the way.

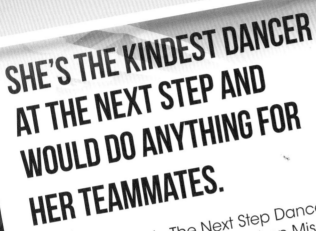

FRIENDS

Despite her bumpy start, **SUMMER** soon became friends with **PIPER**, **JACQUIE** and **KENZIE**. She asked Henry to the prom and they have been close ever since.

DID YOU KNOW?

★ Summer once stepped in to dance for Acro Nation when one of their team was injured.

★ She started dancing at the age of 3!

★ Summer has the longest hair of all the girl dancers (although Henry's might be longer!)

FACT FILE

EYE COLOUR: Blue

HAIR COLOUR: Light brown

MOST LIKELY TO: Be your friend

LEAST LIKELY TO: Stop smiling

FAVOURITE DANCE STYLE: Lyrical and contemporary

THESE NEXT STEP LEGENDS ARE BACK AND IN CHARGE!

Michelle and Emily have been together for a long time. It took a while for Emily to warm up to Michelle at the beginning – Emily was the Queen Bee of A-Troupe when Michelle walked in off the street to audition, and win a spot on the team.

Michelle and Emily argued over dance, friends, boys and the studio. However, they eventually realised that they were much more powerful together than apart. Emily has brains and determination, while Michelle is creative and nurturing. They make the perfect Studio Heads – as long as they don't argue!

MICHELLE

EYE COLOUR: Brown

HAIR COLOUR: Blonde

MOST LIKELY TO: Dance her heart out

LEAST LIKELY TO: Date Eldon again

FAVOURITE DANCE STYLE: Contemporary

MICHELLE AND EMILY

EMILY

EYE COLOUR: Blue

HAIR COLOUR: Blonde

MOST LIKELY TO: Make tough decisions

LEAST LIKELY TO : Go back to making smoothies

FAVOURITE DANCE STYLE: Contemporary

DID YOU KNOW?

Michelle and Emily both dated Eldon. They now both agree that dating him was probably a big mistake!

They were once in charge of competing sides of the studio: TNS East and TNS West.

PART FOUR

NOAH'S DILEMMA
REGIONALS

It is time for Regionals. Although Noah has been to plenty of competitions before, something about this one feels different. Perhaps it's because it might be his last time performing with the team.

As Dance Captain it is up to Noah to lift everyone's spirits and get them excited for their first dance – the hip-hop routine.

The routine goes well, wowing the judges and the audience.

Despite this, Piper isn't herself. She still isn't confident with her aerials, even with the extra practice she has put in. But the contemporary routine is next, and it is too late to change the choreography now. The routine starts off brilliantly.

When the time comes for her aerial, Piper misses her landing and falls. Her mistake sends The Next Step into 7th place. With only the top three studios moving onto the next round, everything is riding on the ballet duet. Noah isn't about to give up yet.

Noah pulls Richelle to one side before the routine. Holding back tears, he tells her that this could be the last time they dance together.

Richelle is scared about losing one of her oldest friends, but she agrees to put her whole heart into the dance.

Noah and Richelle's dance mesmerises the judges and everyone in the wings. They perform the routine the best they ever have – and the magic they create on stage works. The Next Step moves from 7th to 3rd place, and into the next round.

There is only one dance to go. But first, Noah has to talk to Jacquie. He has realised that he needs to leave The Next Step and discover what is in store for him outside the walls of the studio. Noah hopes that Jacquie will support him, and that they can still be together.

There is still one dance left for Noah and The Next Step. Can he pull the team together and win Regionals before he says goodbye? He gets everyone together for one final pep-talk.

The routine features the dancers as black and white piano keys. Noah is dressed in red, and is trying to set them all free. Slowly, the dancers' outfits turn red to match Noah's, and they all dance in unison.

Jacquie shakes her head at Noah. Smiling through tears, she tells him that they can't be together – she can't hold him back. Noah nods. He knows Jacquie is right. Even if it breaks his heart.

After the amazing performance, the judges announce The Next Step as the winners. Emily and Michelle run on stage to hug their team. As everyone jumps for joy, Noah is both happy and sad. He is leaving behind everything he knows, but what lies ahead is an exciting mystery.

ACROBATICS

ACRO IS ONE OF THE MOST PHYSICALLY DEMANDING STYLES OF DANCE, AND CAN BE SPECTACULAR TO WATCH.

WHAT IS IT?

Although it might be one of the less well known forms of dance, acro has been around since the 1900s. It combines gymnastic moves with contemporary and jazz dance styles. A lot of professional performers use acro in their acts, including the world-famous Cirque du Soleil.

WHAT'S SO GREAT?

Acro dances can be mesmerising and exciting to watch. Dancers are able to bend into different positions and use their bodies to create incredible lines and shapes.

WHAT'S TRICKY?

To be a great acro dancer you need to be good at both dance and gymnastics. If you think you'd like to be an acro dancer, try learning gymnastics as well as dance to get your skills and strength up.

TOP ACRO TIPS

1 Be patient. Acro skills won't come overnight – they take a lot of time to perfect. You need to train your body to move in ways it's not really supposed to.

2 Stretch and warm up. Acro dancers do lots of bending, which won't be possible if your muscles are cold.

3 Get help. The best way to learn acro is from a professional, so check out classes that are near you.

TOP MOVE

RIDGE

...is move is one of the first ...oves gymnasts attempt. ...ake sure you stretch out ...ur arms and legs for at ...ast one minute before ...ving it a go. If you can't ...o it straight away, don't ...orry. To make a bridge ...ur back needs to be flexible, and your arms and legs need to be strong, so this can take time and practice to perfect!

1 Start by lying on your back (it's best to do this on a gymnastics or yoga mat, if you have one).

2 Draw your knees up so that your ankles are about ten centimetres from your bottom. Make sure your feet are planted firmly on the ground!

3 Next, bring your hands up beside your ears so that your palms are flat on the ground and your fingers are pointing towards your feet.

4 Now, push your tummy and bottom upwards, using the power from your arms and legs, until you have formed a bridge shape.

TOP TIP!
If you are struggling, try moving your feet a little further apart to help you balance.

THE COOL DOWN

Taking the time to relax and recover after dancing is very important. Dancers take great care of their muscles and feet, and always make sure they eat well!

THE POWER OF STRETCH

Stretching is a great way to stop your muscles from seizing up after dancing. Try these three stretches:

1. Sit on the floor with your legs straight out in front of you. Gently lean forwards to reach your toes. If this feels painful, bend your legs slightly. You should feel a stretch in the back of your legs.

2. Stand with your legs hip-width apart and place your hands on your hips. Slowly bend to your left side until you feel a stretch down your right side. Repeat this, bending to the other side.

3. Stand straight. Raise your arms straight above your head and clasp your hands together. Gently bend backwards to give your lower back a small stretch.

TREAT YOUR FEET!

Give your feet a well-earned pamper with these easy steps.

1. Trim your nails and take off any old nail polish.

2. Fill a large bowl (a washing up bowl works well!) with warm water. Add three tablespoons of baking soda and stir. If you have any essential oils like bergamot or lavender, add these too.

3. Soak your feet for at least 30 minutes (the perfect amount of time to watch an episode of The Next Step!).

4. Dry your feet gently with a fluffy towel. Then rub in some moisturiser.

5. Pop on a pair of slipper socks.

PAMPER YOUR FACE

Reward your skin after all of that stage make-up with a nourishing home-made face mask.

1. Mash half an avocado in a bowl.
2. Stir in one tablespoon of honey.
3. Add in a handful of oats.
4. Apply all over your face (not too close to your eyes!), and leave on for 15 minutes before washing off with warm water.

MAKE SURE YOU DO A PATCH TEST BEFORE APPLYING YOUR FACE MASK, TO SEE HOW YOUR SKIN WILL REACT.

GOLDEN RULES

EAT WELL

...ating well doesn't have to be boring, just balanced. Eating ...ve portions of fruit and ...eg a day, alongside ...carbohydrates (bread, ...otatoes, pasta) and protein ...(cheese, meat, eggs, beans, ...soya) will give your body all ...the power it needs to keep ...dancing.

DRINK

Water is amazing. It helps to lubricate your joints and keeps you hydrated after a workout. Drink at least eight glasses of water a day to stay healthy.

SLEEP

Sleep is one of the nicest things you can do for your body – and it's really easy! Go to bed early and don't look at any screens for at least an hour before you go to sleep. You'll wake up refreshed and ready to take on any choreography that is thrown at you.

67

HOW WELL DO YOU KNOW ... THE NEXT STEP?

THINK YOU KNOW YOUR A-TROUPE FROM YOUR B-TROUPE? CAN YOU REMEMBER WHO HAS DATED WHO?

LET'S FIND OUT

1 What is the name of Piper's big brother?

a. West
b. Daniel
c. James ✓

2 Who has Jacquie NOT dated?

a. Ozzy ✓
b. Henry
c. Noah

3 What is the name of the acro group that sometimes share The Next Step Dance Studio?

a. Acro All Stars
b. Acro Nation ✓
c. Acro Academy

4 Who joined the studio with Miss Angela?

a. Kenzie, Finn and Summer ✓
b. Piper, Richelle and Kingston
c. Ozzy, Amy and Noah

5 What is the name of Richelle's ex-boyfriend?

a. Eddie
b. Edwin
c. Elliot ✓

6 What is the name of the owner of The Next Step Dance Studio?

a. Miss Abigail
b. Miss Suzy
c. Miss Kate ✓

7 How far have The Next Step gone in competitions?

a. Regionals
b. Nationals
c. Internationals ✓

8 What is the current name of the café under the studio?

a. Shakes and Bakes
b. Shakes and Ladders ✓
c. Shakin' all over

What is Noah's special talent?

a. He can sense things ✓ without seeing them

b. He bakes amazing cupcakes

c. He can do a perfect impression of Miss Kate

 What happens to Richelle and Jacquie at the prom?

a. They wanted to go with the same boy

b. Richelle stood on Jacquie's foot while they were dancing

c. They came in the same dress ✓

 What is the name of Jacquie's little sister?

a. Dana

b. Davis ✓

c. Donna

 Who co-commentates on Regionals in Season 6?

a. Giselle

b. Michelle

c. Stephanie

 Which dance move does Piper struggle to get at first?

a. Backflip

b. Aerial ✓

c. Pirouette

 What is the name of Miss Angela's new dance group?

a. Encore

b. Entice

c. Endgame

 Which show did Noah audition for?

a. Robin Hood ✓

b. Peter Pan

c. Billie Elliot

 Where is The Next Step Dance Studio?

a. Ontario

b. Toronto ✓

c. The Rocky Mountains